Lula's Brew

by Elizabeth O. Dulemba

For Stan,
the magical fusion cuisine master!

xist Publishing

Lula's Aunties were witches,
    the wickedest in the land.
So they taught Lula their
        witchety ways
and bewitching spells
        firsthand.

They made Lula study
        night and day
to learn to make magical potions
    that oozed like boogers
and glowed bright green
in ghastly drinks and lotions.

But Lula didn't like to
fly on a broom
or practice magical spells.
She wanted to brew up tasty dishes
with pleasing aromas
and smells.

Lula dreamed of being a chef
in her neighborhood's favorite haunt.
She wanted a four-star bistro,
her very own restaurant.

She studied a stack of cookbooks
she kept hidden under her bed.
And rather than "30 Minute Spells"
she watched food programs instead.

"Lula, your potions don't work," screeched Zelda, Tippy, and Dink. "Try it again. You'll get one right, eventually . . . we think."

"Here's an easy potion,
    even you can't get it wrong.
It turns a child into a mouse,
    and it doesn't take too long.

"You'll need frog eyes
    and lizard tails,
those are easy to find,
    mouse toes
        and broken snails
            and a mole
                from a bat's behind."

Lula pretended to add
the ingredients
just like her Aunties said,
but when they turned the other way,
she added what she liked instead.

When Lula finished her potion,
it steamed with a yummy perfume.
"It smells too good!"
the Aunties cried.
"Lula, go to your room!"

But Tippy took a tiny sip
and suddenly understood.
"Sisters, you should try this,
it really is quite good."

Meanwhile,
The steam snaked up the chimney
and floated through the town,
right through the Mayor's window.
He awoke and sniffed around.

"What is that magical smell?
I must have some right now!"
He didn't get dressed or
brush his teeth.
He ran outside and ...

Wow!

A crowd already filled the street, every person, dog and mouse. They all walked forward in a daze...

straight for the witches' house.

Knock Knock

They beat upon the door.
"Who's there!?" the Aunties cried.
"It's the good people of Rockville.
May we come inside?

Please, won't you let us try a taste
of your delicious smelling stew?
We won't last a day if we don't
and we'll stay right here
'til you do."

"Seconds please," asked Bobby Dee.
Zelda answered with a smirk,
"I'll give you more if you
sweep the floor."
Bobby got right to work!

"Make it again!" the Aunties cried.
"Of course, whenever you want.
On one condition," Lula said.
"I want a restaurant."

The Aunties gathered up
    tables and chairs,
silverware, napkins and frou-frou.
They set them all
    around the house... while Lula
        planned out
            the menu.

Others tried hard to match Lula's style, but her secrets eluded them all. For along with being a famous chef, she was a bit of a witch after all.

Lula's Cafe was a huge success.
The Mayor was Maitre D.'
Reviewers gave Lula
the highest honors
and her own cooking show on TV.

Her dishes were so mesmerizing,
she was featured in
Gourmand Magazine.
They coined a term just for Lula,
"Magical Fusion Cuisine."

"With this brew, people do what we say," the Aunties laughed. "It's true!"
"Excuse me, Aunties," Lula said, "but I made that brew, . . . not you."

Just then a spoon scraped the empty pot. The people looked confused. They dropped their bowls and walked away as if they'd been excused.

The Mayor begged, "I'd like more too."
Dink said, "Obey my wishes."
"Of course," the Mayor widely grinned
and started scrubbing dishes!

About the Author/Illustrator

Elizabeth O. Dulemba, also known as "e-e-e," is an award-winning author and/or illustrator of fifteen children's books including such titles as *Soap, soap, soap* and *The 12 Days of Christmas in Georgia*. She enjoys casting spells on her children's book community in her roles as Illustrator Coordinator for the Society of Children's Book Writers and Illustrators southern region, as a board member for the Georgia Center for the Book, as a writing and illustration instructor at various universities and venues, and by speaking regularly at schools and events where she mesmerizes her audiences. Her "Coloring Page Tuesday" images garner over a million spooky visitors to her blog annually, and she has over 3,000 subscribers to her weekly newsletter.

To download Lula-themed coloring pages, word find puzzles, computer wallpaper and the actual ghoulish recipe for Lula's brew, visit www.dulemba.com.

Made in the USA
Charleston, SC
31 January 2015